To:

A-FRIEND

From:

A-FRIEND

Message:

ENJOY!!

Published by Christian Art Publishers
PO Box 1599, Vereeniging, 1930, RSA

© 2019
First edition 2019

Designed by Christian Art Publishers

Images used under license from Shutterstock.com

Scripture quotations are taken from the *Holy Bible,*
New Living Translation, copyright © 1996, 2004, 2015 by
Tyndale House Foundation. Used by permission of
Tyndale House Publishers, Inc., Carol Stream, Illinois 60188.
All rights reserved.

Scripture taken from the *Holy Bible*, New International Version®,
NIV® Copyright © 1973, 1978, 1984, 2011 by Biblica, Inc.®
Used by permission. All rights reserved worldwide.

Scripture taken from the New King James Version®.
Copyright © 1982 by Thomas Nelson. Used by permission.
All rights reserved.

Scripture quotations are from the Holy Bible,
English Standard Version®. ESV® Text Edition: 2016.
Copyright © 2001 by Crossway, a publishing ministry of
Good News Publishers. Used by permission. All rights reserved.

Printed in China

ISBN 978-1-4321-3084-8

19 20 21 22 23 24 25 26 27 28 – 10 9 8 7 6 5 4 3 2 1

THE
Amazing
Grace
PROMISE BOOK

CHRISTIAN ART PUBLISHERS

Amazing Grace!

How sweet the sound
that saved a wretch like me!
I once was lost, but now am found;
was blind, but now I see.

'Twas grace that taught my heart to fear,
and grace my fears relieved;
how precious did that grace appear
the hour I first believed.

Through many dangers, toils and snares,
I have already come;
'tis grace hath brought me safe thus far,
and grace will lead me home.

The Lord has promised good to me,
His Word my hope secures;
He will my Shield and Portion be,
as long as life endures.

Yea, when this flesh and heart shall fail,
and mortal life shall cease,
I shall possess, within the veil,
a life of joy and peace.

The earth shall soon dissolve like snow,
the sun forbear to shine;
but God, who called me here below,
will be forever mine.

When we've been there
ten thousand years,
bright shining as the sun,
we've no less days to
sing God's praise
than when we'd first begun.

JOHN NEWTON

Contents

Amazing
Grace

How sweet the sound
that **saved**
a wretch like me!

I once was lost,

but now am found;
was blind,
but now I see.

1 God's Amazing Grace

To each one of us grace has been
given as Christ apportioned it.

Ephesians 4:7 NIV

"My grace is sufficient for you,
for My power is made perfect in weakness."

2 Corinthians 12:9 ESV

Let us then approach God's throne
of grace with confidence, so that we may
receive mercy and find grace
to help us in our time of need.

Hebrews 4:16 NIV

God saved you by His grace when
you believed. And you can't take credit
for this; it is a gift from God.

Ephesians 2:8 NLT

From His abundance we have
all received one gracious
blessing after another.

John 1:16 NLT

God is able to make all grace abound
to you, so that having all sufficiency
in all things at all times, you may
abound in every good work.

2 Corinthians 9:8 ESV

You no longer live under
the requirements of the law.
Instead, you live under
the freedom of God's grace.

Romans 6:14 NLT

Through Him we have also obtained
access by faith into this grace in which
we stand, and we rejoice in hope
of the glory of God.

Romans 5:2 ESV

The LORD is compassionate
and gracious, slow to anger,
abounding in love.

Psalm 103:8 NIV

We praise God for the glorious
grace He has poured out on us
who belong to His dear Son.

Ephesians 1:6 NLT

For the grace of God has appeared,
bringing salvation for all people.

Titus 2:11 ESV

We are all saved the same way,
by the undeserved grace
of the Lord Jesus.

Acts 15:11 NLT

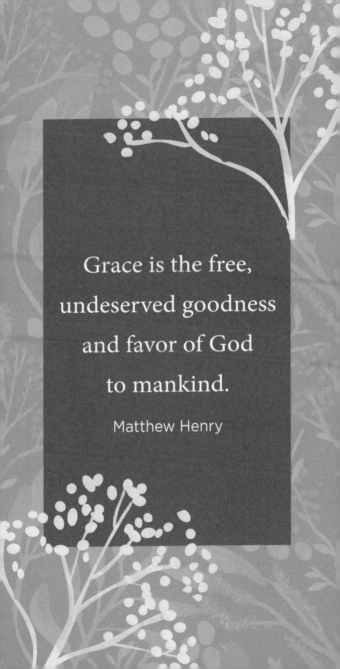

Grace is the free, undeserved goodness and favor of God to mankind.

Matthew Henry

I commend you to God and to
the word of His grace, which is able
to build you up and to give you
the inheritance among all those
who are sanctified.

Acts 20:32 ESV

You know the generous grace of our
Lord Jesus Christ. Though He was rich,
yet for your sakes He became poor,
so that by His poverty
He could make you rich.

2 Corinthians 8:9 NLT

May our Lord Jesus Christ Himself and
God our Father, who loved us and by His
grace gave us eternal encouragement
and good hope, encourage your hearts
and strengthen you in every
good deed and word.

2 Thessalonians 2:16-17 NIV

Even before I was born, God chose me
and called me by His marvelous grace.

Galatians 1:15 NLT

May you experience the love of Christ, though it is too great to understand fully. Then you will be made complete with all the fullness of life and power that comes from God.

Ephesians 3:19 NLT

The God of all grace, who called you to His eternal glory in Christ, after you have suffered a little while, will Himself restore you and make you strong, firm and steadfast.

1 Peter 5:10 NIV

The LORD will give grace and glory; no good thing will He withhold from those who walk uprightly.

Psalm 84:11 NKJV

Because of His grace He declared us righteous and gave us confidence that we will inherit eternal life.

Titus 3:7 NLT

2
The Sweet Sound of Salvation

So prepare your minds for action and exercise self-control. Put all your hope in the gracious salvation that will come to you when Jesus Christ is revealed to the world.

1 Peter 1:13 NLT

Sing to the Lord, bless His name; proclaim the good news of His salvation from day to day.

Psalm 96:2-3 NKJV

If we walk in the light, as He is in the light, we have fellowship with one another, and the blood of Jesus His Son cleanses us from all sin.

1 John 1:7 NIV

I trust in Your unfailing love. I will rejoice because You have rescued me. I will sing to the Lord because He has been so good to me.

Psalm 13:5-6 NLT

"Most assuredly, I say to you, I am
the door of the sheep. All who ever
came before Me are thieves and robbers,
but the sheep did not hear them.
I am the door. If anyone enters by Me,
he will be saved, and will go in and out
and find pasture. The thief does not
come except to steal, and to kill,
and to destroy. I have come that they
may have life, and that they may have it
more abundantly."

John 10:7-10 NKJV

Praise be to the Lord, to God our Savior,
who daily bears our burdens. Our God
is a God who saves; from the Sovereign
LORD comes escape from death.

Psalm 68:19-20 NIV

In Him we have redemption through
His blood, the forgiveness of sins,
in accordance with the riches of
God's grace that He lavished on us.

Ephesians 1:7-8 NIV

Jesus is the stone that was rejected by you, the builders, which has become the cornerstone. And there is salvation in no one else, for there is no other name under heaven given among men by which we must be saved."

Acts 4:11-12 ESV

The Lord takes pleasure in His people; He will beautify the humble with salvation.

Psalm 149:4 NKJV

"I tell you the truth, those who listen to My message and believe in God who sent Me have eternal life. They will never be condemned for their sins, but they have already passed from death into life."

John 5:24 NLT

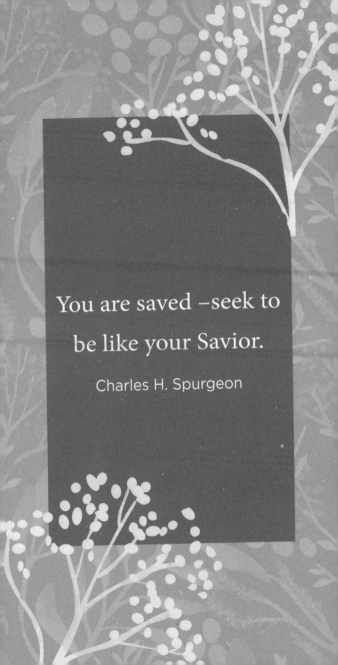

You are saved —seek to be like your Savior.

Charles H. Spurgeon

For there is no distinction between
Jew and Greek, for the same Lord
over all is rich to all who call upon Him.
For "whoever calls on the name
of the Lᴏʀᴅ shall be saved."

Romans 10:12-13 NKJV

I delight greatly in the Lᴏʀᴅ; my soul
rejoices in my God. For He has clothed
me with garments of salvation and
arrayed me in a robe of righteousness.

Isaiah 61:10 NIV

It is good that one should hope
and wait quietly for the salvation
of the Lᴏʀᴅ.

Lamentations 3:26 NKJV

Restore to me the joy
of Your salvation and grant me
a willing spirit, to sustain me.

Psalm 51:12 NIV

Believe in the Lord Jesus, and you
will be saved, you and your household.

Acts 16:31 ESV

If you openly declare that Jesus is Lord
and believe in your heart that God raised
Him from the dead, you will be saved.
For it is by believing in your heart that
you are made right with God, and it is by
openly declaring your faith that
you are saved.

Romans 10:9-10 NLT

He is able to save to the uttermost
those who draw near to God through
Him, since He always lives to make
intercession for them.

Hebrews 7:25 ESV

God says, "At just the right time, I heard
you. On the day of salvation, I helped
you." Indeed, the "right time" is now.
Today is the day of salvation.

2 Corinthians 6:2 NLT

Amazing
Grace

'Twas **grace** that
taught my heart to fear,
and **grace**
my fears relieved;

how precious
did that grace appear
the hour I first
believed.

Since we are receiving a Kingdom
that is unshakable, let us be
thankful and please God by worshiping
Him with holy fear and awe.
For our God is a devouring fire.

Hebrews 12:28-29 NLT

Be sure to fear the LORD and serve Him
faithfully with all your heart; consider
what great things He has done for you.

1 Samuel 12:24 NIV

In mercy and truth atonement
is provided for iniquity; and by the fear
of the LORD one departs from evil.

Proverbs 16:6 NKJV

Honor all people. Love the brotherhood.
Fear God.

1 Peter 2:17 NKJV

"I tell you, My friends, do not be
afraid of those who kill the body and
after that can do no more. But I will show
you whom you should fear:
Fear Him who, after your body has been
killed, has authority to throw
you into hell. Yes, I tell you, fear Him."

Luke 12:4-5 NIV

From the throne came a voice saying,
"Praise our God, all you His servants,
you who fear Him, small and great."

Revelation 19:5 ESV

"Do not curse the deaf or put a
stumbling block in front of the blind,
but fear your God. I am the Lord."

Leviticus 19:14 NIV

How joyful are those who fear the Lord –
all who follow His ways! You will enjoy
the fruit of your labor. How joyful and
prosperous you will be!

Psalm 128:1-2 NKJV

Reverence for the LORD is pure,
lasting forever. The laws of the LORD
are true; each one is fair.

Psalm 19:9 NLT

The fear of the LORD is the beginning
of wisdom; a good understanding have
all those who do His commandments.
His praise endures forever.

Psalm 111:10 NKJV

The LORD takes pleasure in those who
fear Him, in those who hope in
His steadfast love.

Psalm 147:11 ESV

The angel of the LORD encamps
all around those who fear Him,
and delivers them.

Psalm 34:7 NKJV

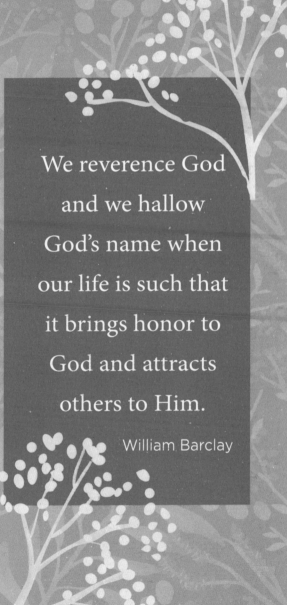

We reverence God and we hallow God's name when our life is such that it brings honor to God and attracts others to Him.

William Barclay

Do not be wise in your own eyes;
fear the Lord and depart from evil.

Proverbs 3:7 NKJV

Let the whole world fear the Lord,
and let everyone stand in awe of Him.
For when He spoke, the world began!
It appeared at His command.

Psalm 33:8-9 NLT

Fear the Lord, you His godly people,
for those who fear Him will have
all they need.

Psalm 34:9 NLT

Let us purify ourselves from everything
that contaminates body and spirit,
perfecting holiness out of
reverence for God.

2 Corinthians 7:1 NIV

Serve only the Lord your God
and fear Him alone. Obey His commands,
listen to His voice, and cling to Him.

Deuteronomy 13:4 NLT

The Mighty One has done great things
for me – holy is His name. His mercy
extends to those who fear Him,
from generation to generation.

Luke 1:49-50 NIV

"Do not be afraid of those who kill the
body but cannot kill the soul. Rather, be
afraid of the One who can destroy
both soul and body in hell."

Matthew 10:28 NIV

Fear God and keep His commandments,
for this is the whole duty of man.

Ecclesiastes 12:13 ESV

Whoever fears the Lord has a secure
fortress, and for their children it will
be a refuge. The fear of the Lord
is a fountain of life, turning a person
from the snares of death.

Proverbs 14:26-27 NIV

He will cover you with His pinions,
and under His wings you will find refuge;
His faithfulness is a shield and buckler.
You will not fear the terror of the night,
nor the arrow that flies by day, nor the
pestilence that stalks in darkness, nor the
destruction that wastes at noonday.

Psalm 91:4-6 ESV

The LORD is my light and my salvation;
whom shall I fear? The LORD is the strength
of my life; of whom shall I be afraid?

Psalm 27:1 NKJV

Even though I walk through the valley
of the shadow of death, I will fear no evil,
for You are with me; Your rod and
Your staff, they comfort me.

Psalm 23:4 NIV

Be strong, and do not fear, for your
God is coming to destroy your
enemies. He is coming to save you.

Isaiah 35:4 NLT

"For I am the Lord your God who takes
hold of your right hand and says to you,
'Do not fear; I will help you.'"

Isaiah 41:13 NIV

When I am afraid,
I will put my trust in You.

Psalm 56:3 NLT

Be strong and courageous. Do not be
afraid or terrified because of them,
for the Lord your God goes with you;
He will never leave you nor forsake you.

Deuteronomy 31:6 NIV

God is our refuge and strength,
an ever-present help in trouble.

Psalm 46:1 NIV

"Have I not commanded you? Be strong
and courageous. Do not be frightened,
and do not be dismayed, for the Lᴏʀᴅ
your God is with you wherever you go."

Joshua 1:9 ESV

We can say with confidence,
"The Lᴏʀᴅ is my helper, so I will have no
fear. What can mere people do to me?"

Hebrews 13:6 NLT

The fear of man brings a snare,
but whoever trusts in the Lᴏʀᴅ
shall be safe.

Proverbs 29:25 NKJV

"So do not fear, for I am with you;
do not be dismayed, for I am your God."

Isaiah 41:10 NIV

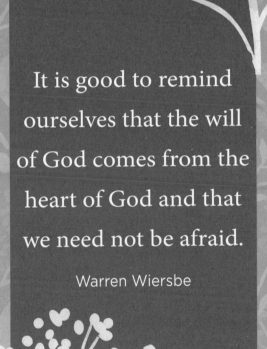

It is good to remind ourselves that the will of God comes from the heart of God and that we need not be afraid.

Warren Wiersbe

God has not given us a spirit of fear
and timidity, but of power, love,
and self-discipline.

2 Timothy 1:7 NLT

I sought the LORD, and He answered me
and delivered me from all my fears.

Psalm 34:4 ESV

There is no fear in love. But perfect love
drives out fear, because fear has to do
with punishment. The one who fears is
not made perfect in love.

1 John 4:18 NIV

"Are not two sparrows sold for a copper
coin? And not one of them falls to the
ground apart from your Father's will.
But the very hairs of your head are all
numbered. Do not fear therefore; you are
of more value than many sparrows."

Matthew 10:29-31 NKJV

Out of my distress I called on the LORD;
the LORD answered me and set me free.
The LORD is on my side; I will not fear.
What can man do to me?

Psalm 118:5-6 ESV

Cast all your anxiety on Him
because He cares for you.

1 Peter 5:7 NIV

All who are led by the Spirit of God
are children of God. So you have not
received a spirit that makes you fearful
slaves. Instead, you received God's Spirit
when He adopted you as His own
children. Now we call Him,
"Abba, Father."

Romans 8:14-15 NLT

In God (I will praise His word), in God
I have put my trust; I will not fear.
What can flesh do to me?

Psalm 56:4 NKJV

Because of Christ and our faith in Him,
we can now come boldly and confidently
into God's presence.

Ephesians 3:12 NLT

Then Jesus told them, "I tell you the
truth, if you have faith and don't doubt,
you can do things like this and much
more. You can even say to this mountain,
'May you be lifted up and thrown
into the sea,' and it will happen."

Matthew 21:21 NLT

We fix our eyes not on what is seen, but
on what is unseen, since what is seen is
temporary, but what is unseen is eternal.

2 Corinthians 4:18 NIV

"I tell you the truth, if you had faith even
as small as a mustard seed, you could
say to this mountain, 'Move from here
to there,' and it would move.
Nothing would be impossible."

Matthew 17:20 NLT

Be on your guard; stand firm in
the faith; be courageous; be strong.

1 Corinthians 16:13 NIV

Now faith is the substance of things
hoped for, the evidence
of things not seen.

Hebrews 11:1 NKJV

Trust in the LORD with all your heart;
do not depend on your own understanding.
Seek His will in all you do, and He will
show you which path to take.

Proverbs 3:5-6 NLT

For in the gospel the righteousness of
God is revealed – a righteousness that is
by faith from first to last, just as it is
written: "The righteous will live by faith."

Romans 1:17 NIV

We live by faith, not by sight.

2 Corinthians 5:7 NIV

What good is it if someone claims to
have faith but has no deeds?
Can such faith save them? Suppose a
brother or a sister is without clothes and
daily food. If one of you says to them,
"Go in peace; keep warm and well fed,"
but does nothing about their physical
needs, what good is it? In the same way,
faith by itself, if it is not accompanied
by action, is dead.

James 2:14-17 NIV

Make every effort to supplement your
faith with virtue, and virtue with
knowledge, and knowledge with
self-control, and self-control with
steadfastness, and steadfastness with
godliness, and godliness with
brotherly affection, and
brotherly affection with love.

2 Peter 1:5-7 ESV

Jesus said, "All things are possible
for one who believes."

Mark 9:23 ESV

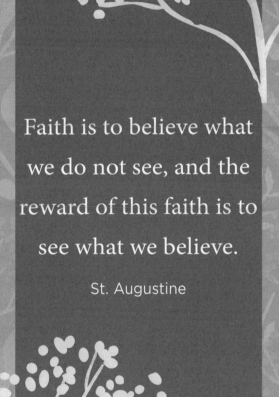

Faith is to believe what we do not see, and the reward of this faith is to see what we believe.

St. Augustine

Be truly glad. There is wonderful joy
ahead, even though you must endure
many trials for a little while.
These trials will show that your faith is
genuine. It is being tested as fire tests
and purifies gold – though your faith is
far more precious than mere gold.
So when your faith remains strong
through many trials, it will bring you
much praise and glory and honor
on the day when Jesus Christ is
revealed to the whole world.

1 Peter 1:6-7 NLT

Faith comes from hearing the message,
and the message is heard through
the word about Christ.

Romans 10:17 NIV

Without faith it is impossible
to please Him, for he who comes
to God must believe that He is,
and that He is a rewarder of those
who diligently seek Him.

Hebrews 11:6 NKJV

For I can do everything through Christ, who gives me strength.

Philippians 4:13 NLT

Everyone who believes that Jesus is the Christ has been born of God, and everyone who loves the Father loves whoever has been born of Him.

1 John 5:1 ESV

We know that a person is made right with God by faith in Jesus Christ, not by obeying the law. And we have believed in Christ Jesus, so that we might be made right with God because of our faith in Christ, not because we have obeyed the law. For no one will ever be made right with God by obeying the law.

Galatians 2:16 NLT

I have fought the good fight, I have finished the race, I have kept the faith.

2 Timothy 4:7 NIV

Amazing
Grace

Through many dangers,
toils and snares,
I have **already**
come;

'tis grace hath brought me

safe thus far,

and grace will lead me home.

Blessed is the one who perseveres under trial because, having stood the test, that person will receive the crown of life.

James 1:12 NIV

We rejoice in our sufferings, knowing that suffering produces endurance, and endurance produces character, and character produces hope, and hope does not put us to shame, because God's love has been poured into our hearts through the Holy Spirit who has been given to us.

Romans 5:3-5 ESV

Consider it pure joy, my brothers and sisters, whenever you face trials of many kinds, because you know that the testing of your faith develops perseverance. Let perseverance finish its work so that you may be mature and complete, not lacking anything.

James 1:2-4 NIV

God had planned something better for us.

Hebrews 11:40 NIV

Since He Himself has gone through
suffering and testing, He is able to
help us when we are being tested.

Hebrews 2:18 NLT

I consider that the sufferings of this
present time are not worth comparing
with the glory that is to be revealed to us.

Romans 8:18 ESV

The more we suffer for Christ, the more
God will shower us with His comfort
through Christ.

2 Corinthians 1:5 NLT

As the elect of God, holy and beloved,
put on tender mercies, kindness,
humility, meekness, longsuffering.

Colossians 3:12 NKJV

If you suffer for doing good and you
endure it, this is commendable
before God.

1 Peter 2:20 NIV

Those who suffer according
to God's will should commit
themselves to their faithful Creator
and continue to do good.

1 Peter 4:19 NIV

Beloved, do not think it strange
concerning the fiery trial which is to try
you, as though some strange thing
happened to you; but rejoice to the
extent that you partake of Christ's
sufferings, that when His glory is
revealed, you may also be glad
with exceeding joy.

1 Peter 4:12-13 NKJV

"When you go through deep waters,
I will be with you. When you go through
rivers of difficulty, you will not drown.
When you walk through the fire of
oppression, you will not be burned up;
the flames will not consume you."

Isaiah 43:2 NLT

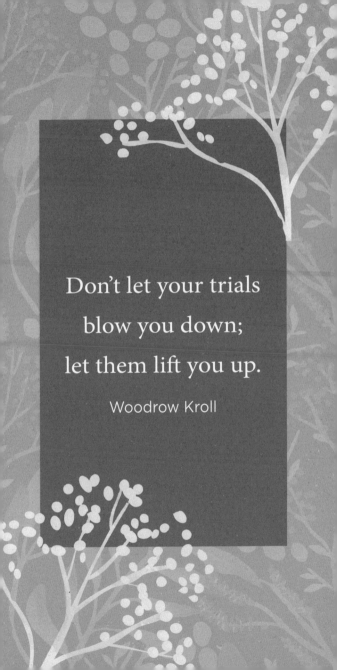

Don't let your trials
blow you down;
let them lift you up.

Woodrow Kroll

Be strong and do not give up,
for your work will be rewarded.

2 Chronicles 15:7 NIV

The Lord knows how to rescue
godly people from their trials.

2 Peter 2:9 NLT

Let us throw off everything that hinders
and the sin that so easily entangles.
And let us run with perseverance
the race marked out for us.

Hebrews 12:1 NIV

"Don't let your hearts be troubled.
Trust in God, and trust also in Me."

John 14:1 NLT

The LORD sustains them on their
sickbed and restores them from
their bed of illness.

Psalm 41:3 NIV

The LORD hears His people
when they call to Him for help.
He rescues them from all their troubles.

Psalm 34:17 NLT

The LORD is a stronghold for
the oppressed, a stronghold in times of
trouble. And those who know Your name
put their trust in You, for You, O LORD,
have not forsaken those who seek You.

Psalm 9:9-10 ESV

Share each other's burdens,
and in this way obey
the law of Christ.

Galatians 6:2 NLT

7 In the Shelter of the Most High

The LORD keeps you from all
harm and watches over your life.
The LORD keeps watch over you as you
come and go, both now and forever.

Psalm 121:7-8 NLT

The name of the LORD is a fortified tower;
the righteous run to it and are safe.

Proverbs 18:10 NIV

The LORD is faithful,
and He will strengthen you
and protect you from the evil one.

2 Thessalonians 3:3 NIV

I will say of the LORD, "He is my refuge
and my fortress; my God,
in Him I will trust."

Psalm 91:2 NKJV

The LORD your God will personally
go ahead of you. He will neither
fail you nor abandon you.

Deuteronomy 31:6 NLT

"I am the LORD your God who takes hold
of your right hand and says to you,
Do not fear; I will help you."

Isaiah 41:13 NIV

With every bone in my body I will praise
Him: "LORD, who can compare with You?
Who else rescues the helpless from the
strong? Who else protects the helpless
and poor from those who rob them?"

Psalm 35:10 NLT

As for me, it is good to be near God.
I have made the Sovereign LORD
my refuge; I will tell of all Your deeds.

Psalm 73:28 NIV

The Lord is my fortress, protecting me from danger, so why should I tremble?

Psalm 27:1 NLT

"Fear not, for I am with you;
be not dismayed, for I am your God;
I will strengthen you, I will help you,
I will uphold you."

Isaiah 41:10 ESV

He renews my strength.
He guides me along right paths,
bringing honor to His name.

Psalm 23:3 NLT

The Lord is on my side; I will not fear.
What can man do to me?

Psalm 118:6 ESV

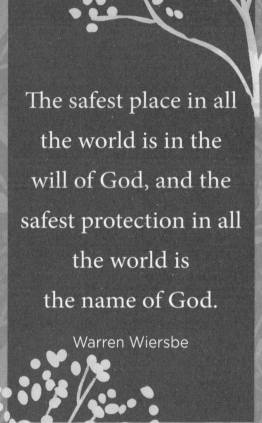

The safest place in all
the world is in the
will of God, and the
safest protection in all
the world is
the name of God.

Warren Wiersbe

The Lord protects all those who love Him,
but He destroys the wicked.

Psalm 145:20 NLT

The Lord protects the unwary;
when I was brought low,
He saved me.

Psalm 116:6 NIV

Let all who take refuge in You rejoice;
let them ever sing for joy, and spread
Your protection over them, that those
who love Your name may exult in You.

Psalm 5:11 ESV

The Lord is a refuge for the oppressed,
a stronghold in times of trouble.

Psalm 9:9 NIV

Show me Your unfailing love in
wonderful ways. By Your mighty power
You rescue those who seek refuge
from their enemies.

Psalm 17:7 NLT

The LORD is the strength of His people;
He is the saving refuge of His anointed.

Psalm 28:8 ESV

The LORD will rescue His servants;
no one who takes refuge in Him
will be condemned.

Psalm 34:22 NIV

The LORD of hosts is with us;
the God of Jacob is our refuge.

Psalm 46:7 NKJV

8 He Leads Us Safely Home

The LORD will guide you always;
He will satisfy your needs in a
sun-scorched land and will strengthen
your frame. You will be like a
well-watered garden, like a spring
whose waters never fail.

Isaiah 58:11 NIV

Jesus said to him, "I am the way,
the truth, and the life. No one comes
to the Father except through Me."

John 14:6 NKJV

Show me Your ways, LORD, teach me
Your paths. Guide me in Your truth and
teach me, for You are God my Savior,
and my hope is in You all day long.

Psalm 25:4-5 NIV

Send out Your light and Your truth;
let them guide me. Let them lead me
to Your holy mountain, to the place
where You live.

Psalm 43:3 NLT

"Call to Me, and I will answer you,
and show you great and mighty things,
which you do not know."

Jeremiah 33:3 NKJV

Your word is a lamp to guide my feet
and a light for my path.

Psalm 119:105 NLT

Teach me to do Your will, for You
are my God! Let Your good Spirit
lead me on level ground!

Psalm 143:10 ESV

May the Lord direct your hearts into
God's love and Christ's perseverance.

2 Thessalonians 3:5 NIV

The LORD directs the steps of the godly.
He delights in every detail of their lives.
Though they stumble, they will never fall,
for the LORD holds them by the hand.

Psalm 37:23-24 NLT

Whether you turn to the right or to the left, your ears will hear a voice behind you, saying, "This is the way; walk in it."

Isaiah 30:21 NIV

The Lord is good and does what is right;
He shows the proper path
to those who go astray.

Psalm 25:8 NLT

Direct my steps by Your word,
and let no iniquity have
dominion over me.

Psalm 119:133 NKJV

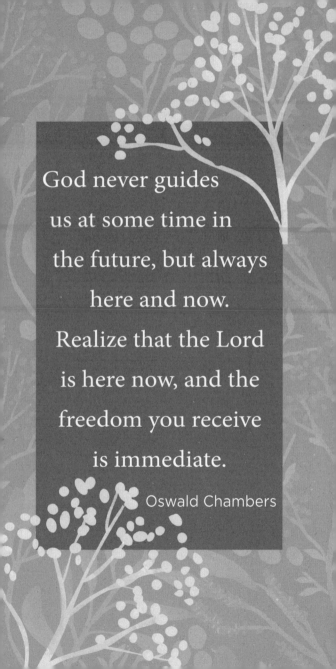

God never guides
us at some time in
the future, but always
here and now.
Realize that the Lord
is here now, and the
freedom you receive
is immediate.

Oswald Chambers

"I will go before you and make
the crooked places straight;
I will break in pieces the gates
of bronze and cut the bars of iron."

Isaiah 45:2 NKJV

God is our God for ever and ever;
He will be our guide even to the end.

Psalm 48:14 NIV

The Lord says, "I will guide you along the
best pathway for your life. I will advise
you and watch over you."

Psalm 32:8 NLT

May He give you the desire of your heart
and make all your plans succeed.

Psalm 20:4 NIV

Put your hope in the LORD.
Travel steadily along His path.

Psalm 37:34 NLT

For the word of the LORD is upright,
and all His work is done in faithfulness.

Psalm 33:4 ESV

He leads the humble in doing right,
teaching them His way.
The LORD leads with unfailing love
and faithfulness all who keep
His covenant and obey His demands.

Psalm 25:9-10 NLT

We can make our plans,
but the LORD determines our steps.

Proverbs 16:9 NKJV

Amazing
Grace

The **Lord**
has promised good to me,

His **Word**
my hope secures;

He will my **Shield**
and **Portion** be,

as long as life endures.

"Blessed are those who hunger
and thirst for righteousness,
for they shall be satisfied."

Matthew 5:6 ESV

May you be blessed by the Lord,
the Maker of heaven and earth.

Psalm 115:15 NIV

The curse of the Lord is on the house
of the wicked, but He blesses
the home of the just.

Proverbs 3:33 NKJV

Blessed are those who trust in the Lord
and have made the Lord their hope
and confidence.

Jeremiah 17:7 NLT

The blessing of the Lord brings wealth,
without painful toil for it.

Proverbs 10:22 NIV

Blessed are those whose way is
blameless, who walk in
the law of the LORD!

Psalm 119:1 ESV

"God blesses those who are poor
and realize their need for Him,
for the Kingdom of Heaven is theirs."

Matthew 5:3 NLT

Taste and see that the LORD is good;
blessed is the one who
takes refuge in Him.

Psalm 34:8 NIV

The LORD will indeed give what is good,
and our land will yield its harvest.

Psalm 85:12 NIV

"Blessed are the pure in heart,
for they shall see God."

Matthew 5:8 NKJV

When You open Your hand,
You satisfy the hunger and thirst
of every living thing. The Lord is
righteous in everything He does;
He is filled with kindness.

Psalm 145:16-17 NLT

"Bring all the tithes into the
storehouse so there will be enough
food in My Temple. If you do," says the
Lord of Heaven's Armies, "I will open the
windows of heaven for you. I will pour
out a blessing so great you won't have
enough room to take it in! Try it!
Put Me to the test!"

Malachi 3:10 NLT

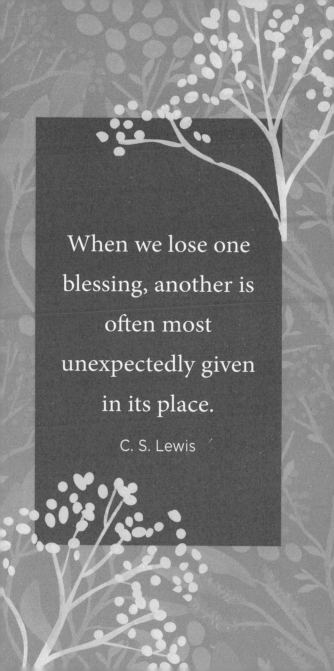

When we lose one
blessing, another is
often most
unexpectedly given
in its place.

C. S. Lewis

The Lord bless you and keep you;
the Lord make His face
shine upon you, and be gracious to you;
the Lord lift up His countenance
upon you, and give you peace.

Numbers 6:24-26 NKJV

"God blesses those who are merciful,
for they will be shown mercy."

Matthew 5:7 NLT

The Lord is my chosen portion
and my cup; You hold my lot.
The lines have fallen for me
in pleasant places; indeed,
I have a beautiful inheritance.

Psalm 16:5-6 ESV

"Blessed are the meek,
for they will inherit the earth."

Matthew 5:5 NIV

All praise to God, the Father of our Lord
Jesus Christ, who has blessed us with
every spiritual blessing in the heavenly
realms because we are united with Christ.

Ephesians 1:3 NLT

You go before me and follow me.
You place Your hand of blessing on my
head. Such knowledge is too wonderful
for me, too great for me to understand!

Psalm 139:5-6 NLT

The LORD your God will bless you in all
your harvest and in all the work of your
hands, and your joy will be complete.

Deuteronomy 16:15 NIV

"I will bless those who have humble and
contrite hearts, who tremble at My word."

Isaiah 66:2 NLT

All Scripture is inspired by God and is useful to teach us what is true and to make us realize what is wrong in our lives. It corrects us when we are wrong and teaches us to do what is right. God uses it to prepare and equip His people to do every good work.

2 Timothy 3:16-17 NLT

Above all, you must understand that no prophecy of Scripture came about by the prophet's own interpretation of things. For prophecy never had its origin in the human will, but prophets, though human, spoke from God as they were carried along by the Holy Spirit.

2 Peter 1:20-21 NIV

Jesus answered, "It is written: 'Man shall not live on bread alone, but on every word that comes from the mouth of God.'"

Matthew 4:4 NIV

For whatever was written
in former days was written for
our instruction, that through endurance
and through the encouragement of the
Scriptures we might have hope.

Romans 15:4 ESV

"Heaven and earth will pass away,
but My words will never pass away."

Matthew 24:35 NIV

For the word of God is alive and active.
Sharper than any double-edged sword,
it penetrates even to dividing soul and
spirit, joints and marrow; it judges the
thoughts and attitudes of the heart.

Hebrews 4:12 NIV

The entirety of Your word is truth,
and every one of Your righteous
judgments endures forever.

Psalm 119:160 NKJV

"Keep this Book of the Law
always on your lips; meditate on it
day and night, so that you may be careful
to do everything written in it. Then
you will be prosperous and successful."

Joshua 1:8 NIV

Blessed are those whose way is blameless,
who walk in the law of the Lord!
Blessed are those who keep His testimonies,
who seek Him with their whole heart,
who also do no wrong,
but walk in His ways!

Psalm 119:1-3 ESV

"Blessed rather are those who hear the
word of God and obey it."

Luke 11:28 NIV

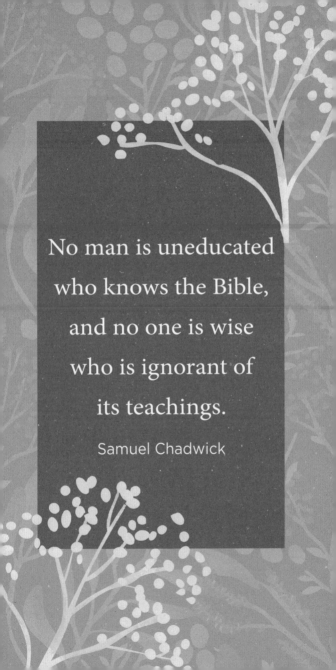

No man is uneducated who knows the Bible, and no one is wise who is ignorant of its teachings.

Samuel Chadwick

Your word, Lord, is eternal;
it stands firm in the heavens.

Psalm 119:89 NIV

The grass withers and the flowers fade,
but the word of our God stands forever.

Isaiah 40:8 NLT

As the Scriptures say, "People are like grass;
their beauty is like a flower in the field.
The grass withers and the flower fades.
But the word of the Lord remains forever."
And that word is the Good News
that was preached to you.

1 Peter 1:24-25 NLT

I will worship toward Your holy temple,
and praise Your name for Your
lovingkindness and Your truth;
for You have magnified Your word
above all Your name.

Psalm 138:2 NKJV

In the beginning was the Word,
and the Word was with God,
and the Word was God.

John 1:1 ESV

The Word became flesh and made His
dwelling among us. We have seen His
glory, the glory of the one and only Son,
who came from the Father,
full of grace and truth.

John 1:14 NIV

We proclaim to you the One who existed
from the beginning, whom we have heard
and seen. We saw Him with our own eyes
and touched Him with our own hands.
He is the Word of life.

1 John 1:1 NLT

The LORD is my strength and shield.
I trust Him with all my heart.
He helps me, and my heart
is filled with joy.

Psalm 28:7 NLT

The LORD is my rock and my fortress and
my deliverer, my God, my rock, in whom
I take refuge, my shield, and the horn
of my salvation, my stronghold.

Psalm 18:2 ESV

You have given me Your shield of victory;
Your help has made me great.

2 Samuel 22:36 NKJV

My flesh and my heart may fail,
but God is the strength of my heart
and my portion forever.

Psalm 73:26 NIV

Through the LORD's mercies
we are not consumed, because
His compassions fail not.
They are new every morning; great is
Your faithfulness. "The LORD is my
portion," says my soul,
"Therefore I hope in Him!"

Lamentations 3:22-24 NKJV

Every word of God is flawless; He is a
shield to those who take refuge in Him.

Proverbs 30:5 NIV

You, O LORD, are a shield around me;
You are my glory, the One who
holds my head high.

Psalm 3:3 NLT

My shield is with God, who saves
the upright in heart.

Psalm 7:10 ESV

He grants a treasure of
common sense to the honest. He is a
shield to those who walk with integrity.

Proverbs 2:7 NLT

You are my refuge and my shield;
I have put my hope in Your word.

Psalm 119:114 NIV

The LORD is my portion; I promise to keep
Your words. I entreat Your favor with all
my heart; be gracious to me according
to Your promise.

Psalm 119:57-58 ESV

I cried out to You, O LORD: I said,
"You are my refuge, my portion
in the land of the living."

Psalm 142:5 NKJV

Our soul waits for the LORD;
He is our help and our shield.

Psalm 33:20 NKJV

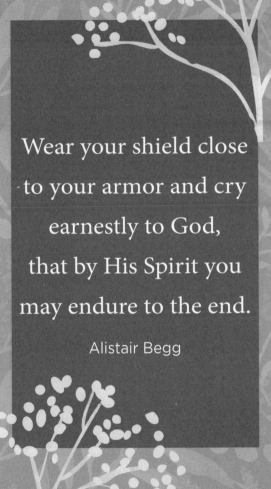

Wear your shield close to your armor and cry earnestly to God, that by His Spirit you may endure to the end.

Alistair Begg

As for God, His way is perfect;
the word of the LORD is proven;
He is a shield to all who trust in Him.

2 Samuel 22:31 NKJV

Let all who take refuge in You rejoice;
let them sing joyful praises forever.
Spread Your protection over them, that
all who love Your name may be filled with
joy. For You bless the godly, O LORD; You
surround them with Your shield of love.

Psalm 5:11-12 NLT

You have given me the shield of Your
salvation, and Your right hand supported
me, and Your gentleness made me great.

Psalm 18:35 ESV

The LORD is my rock, my fortress and my
deliverer; my God is my rock, in whom
I take refuge, my shield and the horn of
my salvation. He is my stronghold,
my refuge and my savior.

2 Samuel 22:2-3 NIV

How blessed you are, O Israel!
Who else is like you, a people saved
by the Lord? He is your protecting
shield and your triumphant sword!
Your enemies will cringe before you,
and you will stomp on their backs!

Deuteronomy 33:29 NLT

Praise be to the Lord my Rock,
who trains my hands for war, my fingers
for battle. He is my loving God and my
fortress, my stronghold and my deliverer,
my shield, in whom I take refuge.

Psalm 144:1-2 NIV

Then the Lord will appear over them;
His arrow will flash like lightning.
The Sovereign Lord will sound the
trumpet; He will march in the storms of
the south, and the Lord Almighty will
shield them. They will destroy and
overcome with slingstones. They will
drink and roar as with wine; they will be
full like a bowl used for sprinkling the
corners of the altar.

Zechariah 9:14-15 NIV

Amazing
Grace

Yea, when this flesh
and **heart** shall fail,

and mortal life shall cease,

I shall possess,
within the veil,

a life of joy
and peace.

This is the day that the Lord has made;
let us rejoice and be glad in it.

Psalm 118:24 ESV

Those who sow with tears
will reap with songs of joy.

Psalm 126:5 NIV

The Lord is my strength and song,
and He has become my salvation.

Psalm 118:14 NKJV

Glory in His holy name; let the hearts of
those who seek the Lord rejoice.

Psalm 105:3 NIV

"Rejoice because your names
are written in heaven."

Luke 10:20 NKJV

"Be happy! Yes, leap for joy! For a great reward awaits you in heaven."

Luke 6:23 NLT

In Him our hearts rejoice,
for we trust in His holy name.

Psalm 33:21 NIV

The joy of the Lord is your strength.

Nehemiah 8:10 NKJV

When Your words came, I ate them;
they were my joy and my heart's delight.

Jeremiah 15:16 NIV

You turned my wailing into dancing;
You removed my sackcloth
and clothed me with joy.

Psalm 30:11 NIV

Those who look to Him for help
will be radiant with joy; no shadow
of shame will darken their faces.

Psalm 34:5 NLT

Because You are my help,
I sing in the shadow of Your wings.

Psalm 63:7 NIV

Enjoy what you have rather than
what you don't have.

Ecclesiastes 6:9 NLT

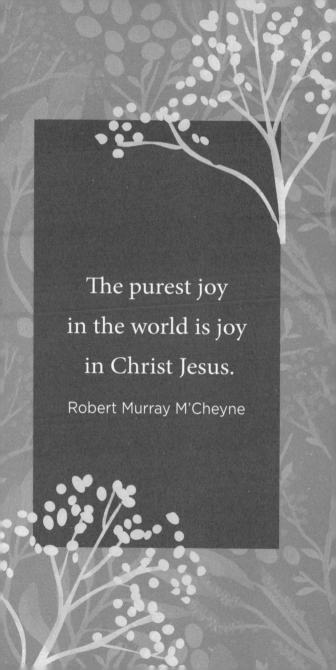

The purest joy
in the world is joy
in Christ Jesus.

Robert Murray M'Cheyne

You have given me greater joy
than those who have abundant harvests
of grain and new wine.

Psalm 4:7 NLT

Light shines on the godly, and joy on
those whose hearts are right.

Psalm 97:11 NLT

Honor and majesty are before Him;
strength and gladness are in His place.

1 Chronicles 16:27 NKJV

Let all those who seek You rejoice
and be glad in You; and let those who
love Your salvation say continually,
"Let God be magnified!"

Psalm 70:4 NKJV

For His anger lasts only a moment, but
His favor lasts a lifetime; weeping may
remain for a night, but rejoicing
comes in the morning.

Psalm 30:5 NIV

The precepts of the Lord are right,
giving joy to the heart.
The commands of the Lord are radiant,
giving light to the eyes.

Psalm 19:8 NIV

The Lord has done great things for us,
and we are filled with joy.

Psalm 126:3 NIV

Shouts of joy and victory resound in the
tents of the righteous: "The Lord's right
hand has done mighty things!"

Psalm 118:15 NIV

"I am leaving you with a gift – peace of mind and heart. And the peace I give is a gift the world cannot give. So don't be troubled or afraid."

John 14:27 NLT

"In Me you may have peace. In the world you will have tribulation; but be of good cheer, I have overcome the world."

John 16:33 NKJV

Jesus said, "Come to Me, all of you who are weary and carry heavy burdens, and I will give you rest."

Matthew 11:28 NLT

"Glory to God in the highest heaven, and on earth peace to those on whom His favor rests."

Luke 2:14 NIV

When people's lives please the LORD,
even their enemies are
at peace with them.

Proverbs 16:7 NLT

The LORD gives strength to His people;
the LORD blesses His people with peace.

Psalm 29:11 NIV

The peace of God, which surpasses all
understanding, will guard your hearts
and your minds in Christ Jesus.

Philippians 4:7 NKJV

Great peace have those who love Your
law, and nothing can make them stumble.

Psalm 119:165 NIV

Let the peace of Christ
rule in your hearts.

Colossians 3:15 ESV

You will keep in perfect peace those
whose minds are steadfast,
because they trust in You!

Isaiah 26:3 NIV

I will both lie down in peace, and sleep;
for You alone, O LORD,
make me dwell in safety.

Psalm 4:8 NKJV

"Blessed are the peacemakers,
for they shall be called sons of God."

Matthew 5:9 ESV

The mind governed by the Spirit
is life and peace.

Romans 8:6 NIV

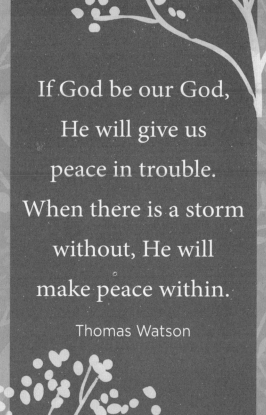

If God be our God,
He will give us
peace in trouble.
When there is a storm
without, He will
make peace within.

Thomas Watson

Submit to God and be at peace
with Him; in this way prosperity
will come to you.

Job 22:21 NIV

Because of God's tender mercy,
the morning light from heaven
is about to break upon us,
to guide us to the path of peace.

Luke 1:78-79 NLT

God is not a God of confusion
but of peace.

1 Corinthians 14:33 ESV

Those who are peacemakers
will plant seeds of peace and
reap a harvest of righteousness.

James 3:18 NLT

The meek will inherit the land and
enjoy peace and prosperity.

Psalm 37:11 NIV

The work of righteousness
will be peace, and the effect of
righteousness, quietness and
assurance forever.

Isaiah 32:17 NKJV

The God of peace be with you.

Romans 15:33 NIV

The kingdom of God is not a matter
of eating and drinking but of
righteousness and peace and joy
in the Holy Spirit.

Romans 14:17 ESV

Amazing
Grace

The **earth**
shall soon dissolve
like snow,
the sun forbear to shine;

but God,
who called me
here below,
will be forever mine.

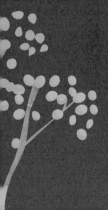

You are a chosen generation,
a royal priesthood, a holy nation,
His own special people,
that you may proclaim the praises
of Him who called you out of darkness
into His marvelous light.

1 Peter 2:9 NKJV

"Before I formed you in the womb
I knew you, before you were born
I set you apart; I appointed you as
a prophet to the nations."

Jeremiah 1:5 NIV

For He chose us in Him before the
creation of the world to be holy and
blameless in His sight. In love He
predestined us for adoption to sonship
through Jesus Christ, in accordance
with His pleasure and will.

Ephesians 1:4-5 NIV

Know that the LORD has set apart
for Himself him who is godly;
the LORD will hear when I call to Him.

Psalm 4:3 NKJV

You have been set apart as holy to the
LORD your God, and He has chosen you
from all the nations of the earth
to be His own special treasure.

Deuteronomy 14:2 NLT

We are His workmanship, created in
Christ Jesus for good works,
which God prepared beforehand
that we should walk in them.

Ephesians 2:10 NKJV

You are a holy people to the LORD
your God; the LORD your God
has chosen you to be a people
for Himself, a special treasure above all
the peoples on the face of the earth.

Deuteronomy 7:6 NKJV

Once you were not a people,
but now you are God's people;
once you had not received mercy,
but now you have received mercy.

1 Peter 2:10 ESV

He is Lord of lords and King of kings;
and those who are with Him
are called, chosen, and faithful.

Revelation 17:14 NKJV

"You did not choose Me,
but I chose you and appointed you
that you should go and bear fruit
and that your fruit should abide,
so that whatever you ask the Father
in My name, He may give it to you."

John 15:16 ESV

To all who did receive Him, who believed
in His name, He gave the right to become
children of God, who were born, not of
blood nor of the will of the flesh nor of
the will of man, but of God.

John 1:12-13 ESV

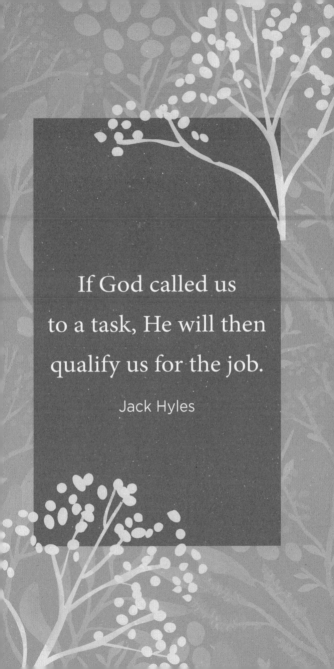

If God called us
to a task, He will then
qualify us for the job.

Jack Hyles

God is faithful, who has called you
into fellowship with His Son,
Jesus Christ our Lord.

1 Corinthians 1:9 NLT

God chose you as firstfruits to be saved
through the sanctifying work of the
Spirit and through belief in the truth.

2 Thessalonians 2:13 NIV

"No one can come to Me unless
the Father who sent Me draws him.
And I will raise him up on the last day."

Psalm 6:44 ESV

The Lord will work out His plans
for my life – for Your faithful love,
O Lord, endures forever.

Psalm 138:8 NLT

Let each person lead the life that the
Lord has assigned to him, and to which
God has called him.

1 Corinthians 7:17 ESV

Remember, dear brothers and sisters, that few of you were wise in the world's eyes or powerful or wealthy when God called you. Instead, God chose things the world considers foolish in order to shame those who think they are wise. And He chose things that are powerless to shame those who are powerful. God chose things despised by the world, things counted as nothing at all, and used them to bring to nothing what the world considers important.

1 Corinthians 1:26-28 NLT

He called you to salvation when we told you the Good News; now you can share in the glory of our Lord Jesus Christ.

2 Thessalonians 2:14 NLT

There is one body and one Spirit, just as you were called in one hope of your calling; one Lord, one faith, one baptism; one God and Father of all, who is above all, and through all, and in you all.

Ephesians 4:4-6 NKJV

"Truly, truly, I say to you,
whoever believes has eternal life."

John 6:47 ESV

Whoever has the Son has life;
whoever does not have the Son of God
does not have life.

1 John 5:12 ESV

"My Father's will is that everyone who
looks to the Son and believes in Him
shall have eternal life."

John 6:40 NIV

"God so loved the world that He gave
His only begotten Son, that whoever
believes in Him should not perish
but have everlasting life."

John 3:16 NKJV

I write these things to you who believe
in the name of the Son of God so that
you may know that you have eternal life.

1 John 5:13 NIV

"Indeed, the time is coming
when all the dead in their graves
will hear the voice of God's Son, and they
will rise again. Those who have done
good will rise to experience eternal life,
and those who have continued in evil
will rise to experience judgment."

John 5:28-29 NLT

"Everyone who lives in Me and believes
in Me will never ever die."

John 11:26 NLT

He who believes in the Son has
everlasting life; and he who does not
believe the Son shall not see life.

John 3:36 NKJV

"I give them eternal life, and they shall
never perish; no one will snatch them out
of My hand. My Father, who has given
them to Me, is greater than all; no one
can snatch them out of My Father's hand.
I and the Father are one."

John 10:28-30 NIV

"You can enter God's Kingdom only through the narrow gate. The highway to hell is broad, and its gate is wide for the many who choose that way.
But the gateway to life is very narrow and the road is difficult,
and only a few ever find it."

Matthew 7:13-14 NLT

For the wages of sin is death, but the free gift of God is eternal life through Christ Jesus our Lord.

Romans 6:23 NLT

Therefore we do not lose heart. Even though our outward man is perishing, yet the inward man is being renewed day by day. For our light affliction, which is but for a moment, is working for us a far more exceeding and eternal weight of glory.

2 Corinthians 4:16-17 NKJV

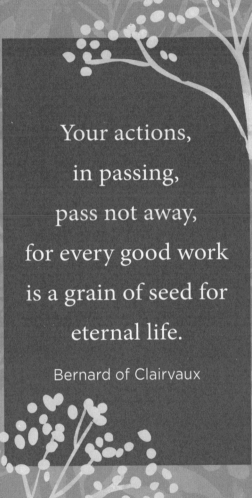

Your actions,
in passing,
pass not away,
for every good work
is a grain of seed for
eternal life.

Bernard of Clairvaux

"Do not work for the food
that perishes, but for the food
that endures to eternal life, which the
Son of Man will give to you. For on
Him God the Father has set His seal."

John 6:27 ESV

"Whoever drinks of this water
will thirst again, but whoever drinks of
the water that I shall give him will never
thirst. But the water that I shall give him
will become in him a fountain of water
springing up into everlasting life."

John 4:13-14 NKJV

"Father, the hour has come.
Glorify Your Son, that Your Son may
glorify You. For You granted Him
authority over all people that He might
give eternal life to all those You have
given Him. Now this is eternal life:
that they know You, the only true God,
and Jesus Christ, whom You have sent."

John 17:1-3 NIV

Do not be deceived:
God is not mocked, for whatever
one sows, that will he also reap.
For the one who sows to his own flesh
will from the flesh reap corruption,
but the one who sows to the Spirit
will from the Spirit reap eternal life.

Galatians 6:7-8 ESV

Because Jesus lives forever, He has a
permanent priesthood. Therefore He is
able to save completely those who come
to God through Him, because He always
lives to intercede for them.

Hebrews 7:24-25 NIV

Where sin increased, grace increased
all the more, so that, just as sin reigned
in death, so also grace might reign
through righteousness to bring eternal
life through Jesus Christ our Lord.

Romans 5:20-21 NIV

Amazing Grace

When we've been there
ten thousand years,
bright **shining**
as the sun,

we've no less days
to sing God's
praise
than when we'd
first begun.

"In My Father's house are many mansions; if it were not so, I would have told you. I go to prepare a place for you. And if I go and prepare a place for you, I will come again and receive you to Myself; that where I am, there you may be also."

John 14:2-3 NKJV

For we know that if the tent that is our earthly home is destroyed, we have a building from God, a house not made with hands, eternal in the heavens.

2 Corinthians 5:1 ESV

"No eye has seen, no ear has heard, and no mind has imagined what God has prepared for those who love Him."

1 Corinthians 2:9 NLT

Jesus answered him, "Truly I tell you, today you will be with Me in paradise."

Luke 23:43 NIV

I heard a loud voice from the throne
saying, "Look! God's dwelling place
is now among the people, and He will
dwell with them. They will be His people,
and God Himself will be with them
and be their God."

Revelation 21:3 NIV

"Then the King will say to those on His
right hand, 'Come, you blessed of
My Father, inherit the kingdom prepared
for you from the foundation of the world:
for I was hungry and you gave Me food;
I was thirsty and you gave Me drink;
I was a stranger and you took Me in;
I was naked and you clothed Me;
I was sick and you visited Me;
I was in prison and you came to Me.'"

Matthew 25:34-36 NKJV

"Not everyone who calls out to Me,
'Lord! Lord!' will enter the Kingdom of
Heaven. Only those who actually do the
will of My Father in heaven will enter."

Matthew 7:21 NLT

"People will come from all over
the world – from east and west,
north and south – to take their places
in the Kingdom of God. And note this:
Some who seem least important now
will be the greatest then, and some who
are the greatest now will be least
important then."

Luke 13:29-30 NLT

God raised us up with Christ and
seated us with Him in the heavenly
realms in Christ Jesus, in order that
in the coming ages He might show the
incomparable riches of His grace,
expressed in His kindness
to us in Christ Jesus.

Ephesians 2:6-7 NIV

"Let the little children come to Me,
and do not forbid them; for of such
is the kingdom of God. Assuredly,
I say to you, whoever does not receive
the kingdom of God as a little child
will by no means enter it."

Mark 10:14-15 NKJV

Let your hope
of heaven master
your fear of death.

William Gurnall

"The kingdom of heaven is like
treasure hidden in a field,
which a man found and covered up.
Then in his joy he goes and sells
all that he has and buys that field."

Matthew 13:44 ESV

He will wipe away every tear from their
eyes, and death shall be no more,
neither shall there be mourning,
nor crying, nor pain anymore, for the
former things have passed away.

Revelation 21:4 ESV

I saw a new heaven and a new earth,
for the first heaven and the first earth
had passed away.

Revelation 21:1 NKJV

"The kingdom of heaven is like a merchant seeking beautiful pearls, who, when he had found one pearl of great price, went and sold all that he had and bought it."

Matthew 13:45-46 NKJV

"Do not lay up for yourselves treasures on earth, where moth and rust destroy and where thieves break in and steal; but lay up for yourselves treasures in heaven, where neither moth nor rust destroys and where thieves do not break in and steal. For where your treasure is, there your heart will be also."

Matthew 6:19-21 NKJV

"Blessed are you who are poor, for yours is the kingdom of God."

Luke 6:20 NIV

Sing praises to God and to His name!
Sing loud praises to Him who rides
the clouds. His name is the LORD –
rejoice in His presence!

Psalm 68:4 NLT

Praise be to the LORD God, the God of
Israel, who alone does marvelous deeds.
Praise be to His glorious name forever;
may the whole earth be filled
with His glory.

Psalm 72:18-19 NIV

I will praise the LORD according to
His righteousness, and will sing praise
to the name of the LORD Most High.

Psalm 7:17 NKJV

Let them praise the name of the LORD,
for His name alone is exalted;
His majesty is above earth and heaven.

Psalm 148:13 ESV

Declare His glory among the nations,
His wonders among all peoples.
For the LORD is great and greatly
to be praised; He is also to be
feared above all gods.

1 Chronicles 16:24-25 NKJV

Praise the LORD! Sing to the LORD
a new song. Sing His praises in
the assembly of the faithful.

Psalm 149:1 NLT

Let heaven and earth praise Him,
the seas and all that move in them.

Psalm 69:34 NIV

I will praise the name of God with a song;
I will magnify Him with thanksgiving.

Psalm 69:30 ESV

Let everything that has breath praise
the LORD. Praise the LORD.

Psalm 150:6 NIV

Praise Him, you highest heavens,
and you waters above the heavens!
Let them praise the name of the LORD!
For He commanded and they were
created. And He established them
forever and ever; He gave a decree,
and it shall not pass away.

Psalm 148:4-6 ESV

Praise the LORD, for the LORD is good;
sing praises to His name,
for it is pleasant.

Psalm 135:3 NKJV

Praise the LORD. Praise the LORD,
you His servants; praise the name
of the LORD. Let the name of the LORD
be praised, both now and forevermore.
From the rising of the sun to the place
where it sets, the name of the LORD
is to be praised.

Psalm 113:1-3 NIV

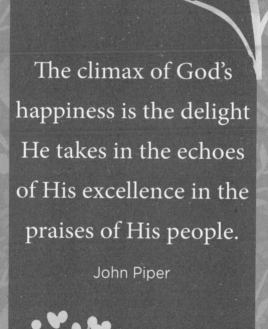

The climax of God's happiness is the delight He takes in the echoes of His excellence in the praises of His people.

John Piper

With all my heart I will praise You,
O Lord my God. I will give glory
to Your name forever, for Your love
for me is very great.

Psalm 86:12-13 NLT

Praise the LORD, my soul; all my inmost
being, praise His holy name. Praise the
LORD, my soul, and forget not all His
benefits – who forgives all your sins and
heals all your diseases, who redeems
your life from the pit and crowns you
with love and compassion.

Psalm 103:1-4 NIV

Sing praises to God, sing praises!
Sing praises to our King, sing praises!
For God is the King of all the earth;
sing praises with a psalm!

Psalm 47:6-7 ESV

Shout to the LORD, all the earth;
break out in praise and sing for joy!

Psalm 98:4 NLT

Let all that I am praise the LORD.
O LORD my God, how great You are!
You are robed with honor and majesty.
You are dressed in a robe of light.

Psalm 104:1-2 NLT

Praise the LORD! I will praise the LORD
with my whole heart, in the assembly
of the upright and in the congregation.
The works of the LORD are great, studied
by all who have pleasure in them.
His work is honorable and glorious,
and His righteousness endures forever.

Psalm 111:1-3 NKJV

Because Your steadfast love is better
than life, my lips will praise You.

Psalm 63:3 ESV

I will exalt You, my God the King;
I will praise Your name for ever and ever.
Every day I will praise You and extol
Your name for ever and ever.

Psalm 145:1-2 NIV

Give thanks to the LORD and proclaim
His greatness. Let the whole world
know what He has done.

Psalm 105:1 NLT

Thanks be to God, who in Christ always
leads us in triumphal procession,
and through us spreads the fragrance
of the knowledge of Him everywhere.

2 Corinthians 2:14 ESV

It is good to give thanks to the LORD,
to sing praises to the Most High.
It is good to proclaim Your unfailing
love in the morning, Your faithfulness
in the evening.

Psalm 92:1-2 NLT

Thanks be to God for His
indescribable gift!

2 Corinthians 9:15 NKJV

Enter His gates with thanksgiving
and His courts with praise;
give thanks to Him and
praise His name.

Psalm 100:4 NIV

Come, let us sing for joy to the LORD;
let us shout aloud to the Rock of our
salvation. Let us come before Him with
thanksgiving and extol Him with music
and song. For the LORD is the great
God, the great King above all gods.

Psalm 95:1-3 NIV

Oh give thanks to the LORD;
call upon His name; make known
His deeds among the peoples!

1 Chronicles 16:8 ESV

May you be filled with joy,
always thanking the Father.

Colossians 1:11-12 NLT

Thank God! He gives us victory
over sin and death through
our Lord Jesus Christ.

1 Corinthians 15:57 NLT

We give thanks to You, O God,
we give thanks! For Your wondrous
works declare that Your name is near.

Psalm 75:1 NKJV

Sing to the LORD with thanksgiving;
sing praises on the harp to our God,
who covers the heavens with clouds,
who prepares rain for the earth, who
makes grass to grow on the mountains.

Psalm 147:7-8 NKJV

You made all the delicate, inner parts
of my body and knit me together in my
mother's womb. Thank You for making
me so wonderfully complex!
Your workmanship is marvelous –
how well I know it.

Psalm 139:13-14 NLT

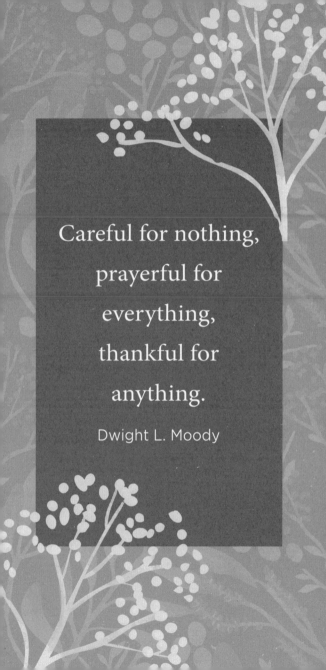

Careful for nothing,
prayerful for
everything,
thankful for
anything.

Dwight L. Moody

I will give thanks to the LORD
with my whole heart; I will recount all
of Your wonderful deeds. I will be glad
and exult in You; I will sing praise
to Your name, O Most High.

Psalm 9:1-2 NLT

Sing and make music from your heart
to the Lord, always giving thanks
to God the Father for everything,
in the name of our Lord Jesus Christ.

Ephesians 5:19-20 NIV

Be thankful in all circumstances,
for this is God's will for you
who belong to Christ Jesus.

1 Thessalonians 5:18 NLT

You are my God, and I will give thanks
to You; You are my God; I will extol You.

Psalm 118:28 ESV

Give thanks to the Lord, for He is good;
His love endures forever.

Psalm 107:1 NIV

"The one who offers thanksgiving as his
sacrifice glorifies Me; to one who orders
his way rightly I will show the
salvation of God!"

Psalm 50:23 ESV

Make thankfulness your sacrifice
to God, and keep the vows
you made to the Most High.

Psalm 50:14 NLT

Whatever you do, in word or deed,
do everything in the name of the
Lord Jesus, giving thanks to
God the Father through Him.

Colossians 3:17 ESV

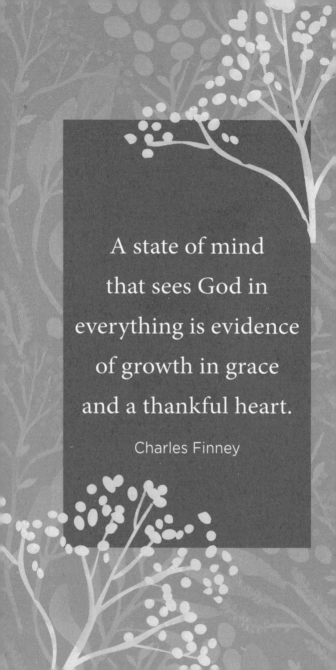

A state of mind
that sees God in
everything is evidence
of growth in grace
and a thankful heart.

Charles Finney